20 SOCCER SUPERSTARS

Mauricio Velázquez de León

WORLD SOCCER BOOKS™

rosen publishing's
rosen central®

New York

Published in 2010 by The Rosen Publishing Group, Inc.
29 East 21st Street, New York, NY 10010

First Edition

Library of Congress Cataloging-in-Publication Data

Velázquez de León, Mauricio.
20 soccer superstars / Mauricio Velazquez de Leon.
   p. cm.–(World soccer books)
Twenty soccer superstars
Includes bibliographical references and index.
ISBN 978-1-4358-9137-1 (library binding)
ISBN 978-1-61532-871-0 (pbk)
ISBN 978-1-61532-872-7 (6 pack)
1. Soccer players–Biography. I. Title.
GV942.7.A1V453 2010
796.334092–dc22

2009020726

Manufactured in China

CPSIA Compliance Information: Batch #HW10YA: For Further Information contact Rosen Publishing, New York, New York at 1-800-237-9932

On the cover: Lionel Messi (Argentina), Cristiano Ronaldo (Portugal), and Marta (Brazil) are three of the best soccer players in the world today.

CONTENTS

INTRODUCTION   **5**

CHAPTER 1   **EMMANUEL ADEBAYOR**   **6**

CHAPTER 2   **DAVID BECKHAM**   **8**

CHAPTER 3   **ALESSANDRO DEL PIERO**   **12**

CHAPTER 4   **LANDON DONOVAN**   **14**

CHAPTER 5   **DIDIER DROGBA**   **16**

CHAPTER 6   **MICHAEL ESSIEN**   **18**

CHAPTER 7   **SAMUEL ETO´O**   **20**

CHAPTER 8   **STEVEN GERRARD**   **22**

CHAPTER 9   **THIERRY HENRY**   **24**

CHAPTER 10   **ZLATAN IBRAHIMOVIĆ**   **28**

CHAPTER 11   **KAKÁ**   **30**

CHAPTER 12   **MIROSLAV KLOSE**   **34**

CHAPTER 13   **RAFAEL MÁRQUEZ**   **36**

CHAPTER 14   **MARTA**   **38**

CHAPTER 15   **LIONEL MESSI**   **41**

CHAPTER 16   **BIRGIT PRINZ**   **44**

CHAPTER 17   **RAÚL**   **46**

CHAPTER 18   **RONALDINHO**   **48**

CHAPTER 19   **CRISTIANO RONALDO**   **52**

CHAPTER 20   **FERNANDO TORRES**   **56**

GLOSSARY   **58**

FOR MORE INFORMATION   **59**

FOR FURTHER READING   **61**

BIBLIOGRAPHY   **62**

INDEX   **63**

INTRODUCTION

Soccer is a team sport. In fact, the sport's official name, association football, implies that the organization, coordination, and relationships among the 11 players on each team are the keys to their success. But in soccer, as with any other team sport, there are players who stand out. Some of them have leadership skills, others may be faster or stronger, and a few more may have a particular technical ability. Some play the game in a different way, moving the ball in an unexpected fashion or creating new tricks. These are the stars of the team, and every team—of the thousands of professional soccer teams around the world—has its own star: an idol, a team symbol. A very small number of these players have something else. They receive the highest awards and play for the most prestigious teams, have made historical plays and scored fantastic goals, and break records and win championships. These are the soccer superstars.

The men and women included in this book come from many different countries and many different backgrounds. Some are great defenders, and others are fantastic playmakers, while plenty of them are goal-scoring specialists. Players like David Beckham and Ronaldinho are well known on and off the field. But others—like Michael Essien, the midfielder from Ghana, and Birgit Prinz, the first lady of German soccer—may not enjoy celebrity status but are among the best soccer players in history.

All of these players have one thing in common: they were all kids who dreamed about becoming soccer players.

Didier Drogba (in blue) heads a ball during a match between Chelsea and Liverpool at the 2009 UEFA Champions League tournament. Drogba moved to France as a child to pursue his dream of playing professional soccer.

EMMANUEL ADEBAYOR

After being nominated twice for African Footballer of the Year, Emmanuel Adebayor finally got the most prestigious award for an African player, and his 30 goals in 48 games with British club Arsenal turned him into one of the most effective scorers in Europe.

Born in Lomé, the capital of Togo, Ade' was discovered at the age of 15 by French team Metz, where he played with the junior side until 2001. The 17 goals he scored during his debut season with the Metz first team earned him a transfer to Monaco, one of the most prestigious clubs in France. Access to the top level of European soccer suited Ade', and in 2004, he helped Monaco reach the UEFA Champions League final. Monaco had a good start in the game against F.C. Porto, but the Portuguese team proved to be superior and won the game 3–0.

A powerful striker with great strength and aerial talent, Adebayor was called in 2006 to fill the space left by French star Thierry Henry in Arsenal. The gunners are one of the most successful teams in England, and the arrival of Adebayor created great expectations. He didn't disappoint. It took him 21 minutes to score his first goal during his debut.

Adebayor is of Nigerian descent, and he had the option to play internationally for soccer powerhouse Nigeria. Instead, he

COUNTRY:
TOGO

FULL NAME:
SHEYI EMMANUEL ADEBAYOR

DATE OF BIRTH:
FEBRUARY 26, 1984

PLACE OF BIRTH:
LOMÉ, TOGO

POSITION:
STRIKER

CLUBS:
SPORTING CLUB DE LOMÉ, METZ, MONACO, ARSENAL

Emmanuel Adebayor lifts his trophy after being named African Footballer of the Year in 2008. Adebayor became a national hero in Togo after helping the team qualify for their first World Cup in 2006.

chose to stay with Togo, the country of his birth and a team without much international success. He scored 11 goals for the Hawks in the qualifying rounds for the 2006 African Cup of Nations and was a key player in the first trip to the 2006 World Cup of this African nation.

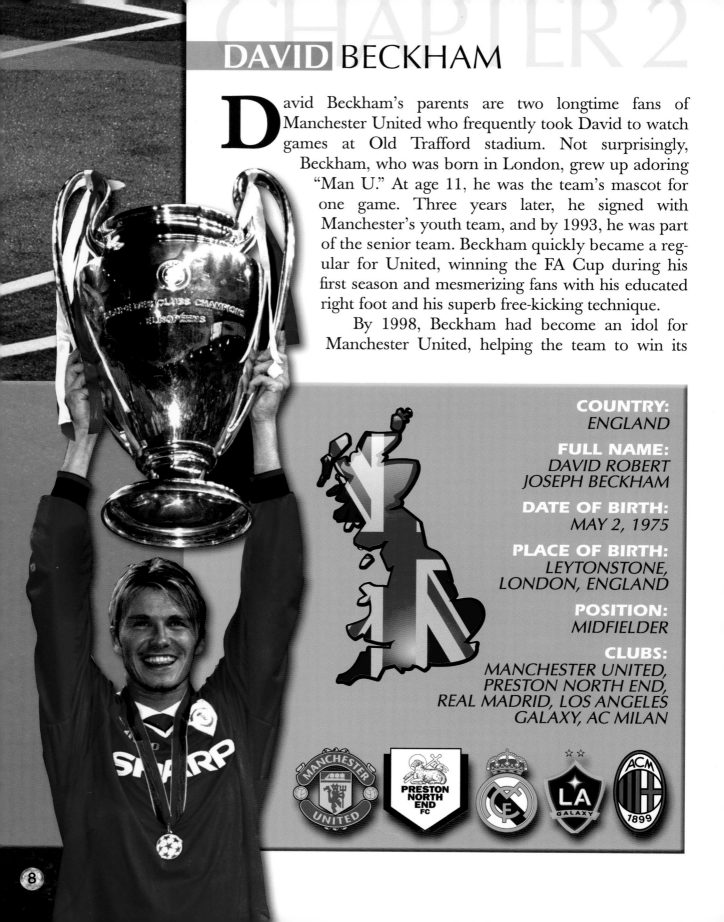

CHAPTER 2

DAVID BECKHAM

David Beckham's parents are two longtime fans of Manchester United who frequently took David to watch games at Old Trafford stadium. Not surprisingly, Beckham, who was born in London, grew up adoring "Man U." At age 11, he was the team's mascot for one game. Three years later, he signed with Manchester's youth team, and by 1993, he was part of the senior team. Beckham quickly became a regular for United, winning the FA Cup during his first season and mesmerizing fans with his educated right foot and his superb free-kicking technique.

By 1998, Beckham had become an idol for Manchester United, helping the team to win its

COUNTRY:
ENGLAND

FULL NAME:
DAVID ROBERT JOSEPH BECKHAM

DATE OF BIRTH:
MAY 2, 1975

PLACE OF BIRTH:
LEYTONSTONE, LONDON, ENGLAND

POSITION:
MIDFIELDER

CLUBS:
MANCHESTER UNITED, PRESTON NORTH END, REAL MADRID, LOS ANGELES GALAXY, AC MILAN

TIMELINE

1992: DEBUTED WITH MANCHESTER UNITED AT THE AGE OF 17.

1999: WON THE UEFA CHAMPIONS LEAGUE WITH MANCHESTER UNITED.

2003: JOINED REAL MADRID.

2003–2004: BECAME GOOGLE'S MOST SEARCHED OF ALL SPORTS TOPICS.

2005: BECAME UNICEF GOODWILL AMBASSADOR.

2007: JOINED LOS ANGELES GALAXY.

2009: BECAME ENGLAND'S MOST-CAPPED OUTFIELD PLAYER WITH 109 APPEARANCES.

first-ever treble by conquering the Premier League, the FA Cup, and the UEFA Champions League. Also in 1998, he started dating one of the Spice Girls, Victoria Adams, and married her a year later. The relationship attracted enormous media attention, and many journalists and fans began to question his commitment to soccer.

The 1998 World Cup in France was Beckham's opportunity to silence his critics, but he was shown a red card for kicking an opponent in a game against Argentina. England was eliminated, and the fans and press blamed Beckham for their fate. Two years later, England was eliminated from the EURO 2000, and British fans mocked Beckham from the stands. Beckham redeemed himself with the national team during the qualifying games of World Cup 2002.

David Beckham lifts the European Cup after Manchester United beat Bayern Munich in the UEFA Champions League in 1999.

DAVID BECKHAM

10

In the last match of the round, England needed to win or draw to qualify for the tournament. But with time running out, England was losing. A foul outside the Greek penalty area awarded a free kick to England, and Beckham made a fantastic kick that curled in midair and landed in the net. England won a trip to the World Cup, and Beckham was again a hero.

During a match three months before the 2002 World Cup in Korea/Japan, Beckham suffered a bad foul that left him with a broken left foot. He was not in great shape during the tournament, but he scored the winning goal against Argentina to advance to the second round. However, England was eliminated in the quarterfinals by Brazil.

In 2003, Beckham joined Real Madrid in Spain. After four seasons without winning any important tournament with Real Madrid, Beckham finally won the 2007 La Liga trophy. Ironically, that would also be his last game with the Spanish team. A few months later, he would sign a contract with the Los Angeles Galaxy in Major League Soccer.

During Beckham's time in Spain, he was called to his national team for the 2006 World Cup. England had a good run but lost again in the quarterfinal stage. Nevertheless, Beckham scored a historic goal against Ecuador, which made him the only British player to score a goal in three consecutive World Cups.

After two seasons with the Galaxy in the United States, Beckham decided that he wanted to be close to the English national team in order to be considered for the qualifying games to World Cup 2010. AC Milan in Italy was happy to arrange a loan-transfer for the British superstar. Beckham was called again for the national team in 2008, and in March 2009, he wore the British jersey for the 108th time, surpassing the legendary Bobby Moore as the British player with the most caps in history.

David Beckham celebrates after scoring the winning goal against Argentina in the 2002 World Cup in Sapporo, Japan. Beckham was England's captain during this tournament.

CHAPTER 3

ALESSANDRO DEL PIERO

When Alessandro Del Piero is on the field, you can feel his energy. This is because not many players own a position on the pitch with the personal playing style of this soccer superstar. A supporting striker, Del Piero moves with elegance in the midfield, assisting many goals and scoring many more. A World Cup champion with Italy and a true idol with team Juventus, Alessandro Del Piero has been named one of FIFA's (Fédération Internationale de Football Association) 125 greatest living footballers.

The son of an electrician and a housekeeper, Del Piero left home at age 13 to play in the youth team of Padova, where he debuted as a professional player in 1991. Two years later, he joined legendary side Juventus, a team where he has become a living icon, playing for more than 16 seasons and becoming their all-time best scorer. Del Piero has lifted seven Serie A trophies, one Intercontinental Cup, and the UEFA Champions League with Juve.

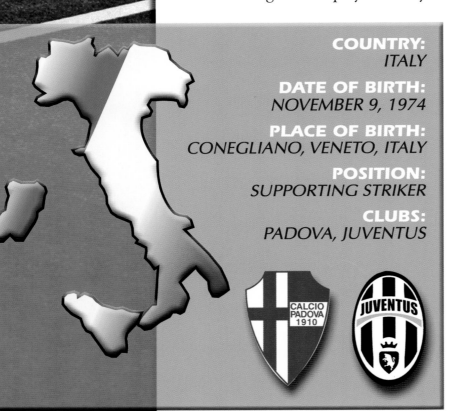

COUNTRY:
ITALY

DATE OF BIRTH:
NOVEMBER 9, 1974

PLACE OF BIRTH:
CONEGLIANO, VENETO, ITALY

POSITION:
SUPPORTING STRIKER

CLUBS:
PADOVA, JUVENTUS

Del Piero was called to join the Italian national team in the shadow of soccer legend Roberto Baggio. After some unremarkable appearances at the EURO 1996 and the 1998 World Cup, Del Piero came from the bench in World Cup 2002 to score the goal that put the Italians in the second round. For World Cup 2006, Del Piero had become a trusted veteran who could help the team in important moments. Once more, he started the tournament on the bench, but he appeared in two of the group

Alessandro Del Piero sprints from two French defenders during the World Cup Germany 2006 final match. Del Piero's experience and skill helped Italy win their fourth World Cup title.

stage matches. He started in Italy's win in the round of 16 but was back on the bench during the semifinal game against Germany. He entered the game near the end of regulation and scored Italy's second goal for the right to play in the final. The final against France ended 1–1 after extra time, and Del Piero scored a penalty in the shoot-out, giving Italy their fourth World Cup.

In 2006, managers from Juventus and other top Italian teams were accused of rigging games by selecting referees. Juventus was downgraded to play in Serie B, and Del Piero showed his loyalty by staying with Juve. In an age where professional players transfer from team to team with great ease, Del Piero's decision was seen as an example of great sportsmanship. In Serie B, Del Piero became top scorer and helped Juventus to return quickly to Serie A. And then, in his first season back in the premier Italian league, Del Piero won his second top scorer award.

CHAPTER 4

LANDON DONOVAN

Landon Donovan is the most talented soccer player in the United States. As the all-time leading scorer and the assist chief for the United States, Donovan is as quick on his feet as he is in his mind, and he's able to change the course of a game with a single stroke.

Donovan grew up in California and was a member of the inaugural class of the U.S. Soccer residency program in Bradenton, Florida, where he was selected for the national team that participated in the 1999 U-17 World Cup. The United States finished fourth, and Donovan won the Golden Ball Award. Donovan's performance attracted the attention of European clubs, and shortly after the World Cup, he became the youngest American player to sign with a foreign team with his contract with Bayer Leverkusen in Germany.

Things did not go well for Donovan in Germany, and he returned to the United States on a loan with the San Jose Earthquakes. Donovan's impact was immediate. He helped the Earthquakes win the MLS Cup in 2001 and 2003. Bayer Leverkusen called Donovan again, and he agreed to give his European adventure a second chance. But after playing only seven scoreless games, Donovan was back in the United States, this time with his home team, the Los Angeles Galaxy.

With Donovan's club career on the rise, his role on the U.S. national team became even more important. He participated in the Olympic team that reached the semifinals in Sydney 2000 and was

COUNTRY:
UNITED STATES

DATE OF BIRTH:
MARCH 4, 1982

PLACE OF BIRTH:
ONTARIO, CALIFORNIA

POSITION:
FORWARD

CLUBS:
BAYER LEVERKUSEN, SAN JOSE EARTHQUAKES, LOS ANGELES GALAXY

a key player in the United States' historical run to the quarterfinals in the 2002 World Cup. Donovan was the most recognized American player going into the 2006 World Cup, and American fans had great hopes for the Californian. Nevertheless, the U.S. team failed to win a single game and were sent home in the first round.

Back with the Los Angeles Galaxy, Donovan recovered quickly, becoming the team's top scorer four years in a row and winning the MLS Golden Boot in 2008. New calls from Europe took him back to Germany, this time to German powerhouse Bayern Munich, but his stay was short. Donovan was back with the Galaxy at the start of the 2009 season.

Landon Donovan is one of the biggest stars of the LA Galaxy and the U.S. National Soccer Team. Many experts agree that Donovan is the most talented soccer player that has ever come from the United States.

CHAPTER 5

DIDIER DROGBA

Didier Drogba came late onto the soccer scene, signing a professional contract at age 21 and having his first successful season at 23. But once he found his form, he became the lethal goal scorer who changed the history of his small West African country.

A powerful striker with a natural instinct for finding the net, Drogba moved to France at the age of five to live with his uncle, a professional soccer player, but it wasn't until he was 15 that he moved permanently with his parents to the suburbs of Paris. At 18, he joined Le Mans in the French Ligue 2, where he struggled to show his talent. Team Guingamp offered him a chance in the Ligue 1, and the Ivorian quickly responded with 20 goals in two seasons. A year later, Drogba joined Marseille, where he became a fan favorite and was selected as Player of the Year in the French League. But it wasn't until July 2004 that Drogba got full international attention with his record transfer to Chelsea, in England.

Drogba's impact in Chelsea was immediate. He took the Blues to win their first-ever Premier League title in 2005, and repeated a year later. Two victories in the League Cup and the 2007 FA Cup cemented Drogba's success in London, and the award as Top Scorer in the Premier League was the perfect reward for him.

COUNTRY:
IVORY COAST

FULL NAME:
DIDIER YVES DROGBA TÉBILY

DATE OF BIRTH:
MARCH 11, 1978

PLACE OF BIRTH:
ABIDJAN, IVORY COAST

POSITION:
STRIKER

CLUBS:
LE MANS, EN AVANT GUINGAMP, MARSEILLE, CHELSEA

Didier Drogba takes control of the ball from Argentina defender Gabriel Heinze during the World Cup Germany 2006. Drogba became the first player from Ivory Coast to score a goal in a World Cup tournament.

In the international arena, Drogba captained Ivory Coast to its first-ever World Cup, in 2006, a feat that turned him into a national hero. He scored the first World Cup goal of his country's history in the opening game against Argentina, but the inexperienced Ivorian team was sent home after two defeats and one victory in the first round. A few months after the World Cup, Drogba was named African Footballer of the Year.

MICHAEL ESSIEN

Michael Essien is a player of great strength and versatility. He can play anywhere on the field. But not many players rule the middle of the pitch with as much authority as this powerful Ghanian.

Essien's introduction to the world stage came in 1999 during the U-17 World Cup in New Zealand. The Black Stars, as the Ghanian national team is known, finished the tournament in third place. Their success opened Europe for Essien, who signed with Sporting Club de Bastia in the French Ligue 2.

A year later, he participated with Ghana in the U-20 World Cup in Argentina, scoring the first goal in the tournament and flying all the way to the final. Ghana lost the final against the host country, but Essien and his teammates continued to impress soccer fans around the world. Back with Bastia, Essien was becoming the talented central midfielder that he is today, and after two seasons in Ligue 2, many top French teams scrambled to sign him. Essien signed with Olympique Lyonnais, where he played two successful seasons, winning the Ligue 1 twice and reaching the quarterfinals in the UEFA Champions League.

In 2005, Essien joined Chelsea in the Premier League and soon took control of the midfield with the Blues. In 2006, Essien helped Chelsea win the Premier League, and in a team filled with stars, he was named Player of the Year. The international stage called again, and Essien played with Ghana in the 2006 World Cup in Germany.

COUNTRY:
GHANA

FULL NAME:
MICHAEL KOJO ESSIEN

DATE OF BIRTH:
DECEMBER 3, 1982

PLACE OF BIRTH:
ACCRA, GHANA

POSITION:
MIDFIELDER

CLUBS:
BASTIA, LYON, CHELSEA

The Black Stars lost the first game with Italy but won their matches against the Czech Republic and the United States, becoming the only African team to advance to the second round. Essien was shown two yellow cards in these games and was suspended for the second-round match against Brazil. The five-time world champions won the game, but the Black Stars were received as heroes back in Ghana. Michael Essien declared that he and his team learned a lot in the World Cup and promised to improve for the 2010 World Cup in South Africa.

Michael Essien is one of the most powerful mid-fielders in the game today. Essien established himself as a player in the French league but became an international star when joining Chelsea in the English Premier League.

CHAPTER 7

SAMUEL ETO'O

W ho was named all-time leading scorer in the history of the African Cup of Nations and named African Footballer of the Year three consecutive times? The name behind these achievements is Samuel Eto'o.

Born in Cameroon, Eto'o started to shine from a young age. He was called to the national team at age 14 and had his official debut a year later. When he played in the 1998 FIFA World Cup, he was the youngest player in the tournament, at the age of 17 years and 3 months. Four years later, in the 2002 World Cup, he scored his first goal in the tournament.

With an outstanding positional awareness, speed, and shooting technique, Eto'o has been a key member of the Cameroon squad during the African Cup of Nations, a tournament they won in 2000 and 2002. He was the leading scorer in the 2008 African Cup of Nations with five goals. He became the all-time scorer in the competition's history with a tally of 16.

After a short stint with the youth squad of Real Madrid, in Spain, and loans to Leganés and Espanyol, Eto'o was transferred to Mallorca in 2000, where he electrified the fans with his quick definition in the penalty area. After four years with Mallorca, Eto'o left the club in 2004,

COUNTRY:
CAMEROON

FULL NAME:
SAMUEL ETO'O FILS

DATE OF BIRTH:
MARCH 10, 1981

PLACE OF BIRTH:
DOUALA, CAMEROON

POSITION
STRIKER

CLUBS:
REAL MADRID, LEGANÉS, ESPANYOL, MALLORCA, FC BARCELONA

Samuel Eto'o salutes his fans after scoring one of his many goals for FC Barcelona. Eto'o is the only player to be named African Footballer of the Year three times in a row.

with the record of most goals scored in a domestic league, and joined legendary team FC Barcelona.

Eto'o won La Liga with Barcelona in his first season and repeated the feat the next year. He put the ball in the net six times during the 2005–2006 UEFA Champions. Barcelona won the championship, and Eto'o was named UEFA's Best Forward of the Year. That same year, he took home his third African Footballer of the Year Award, making him the first player to win the award three years in succession (2003, 2004, and 2005).

CHAPTER 8

STEVEN GERRARD

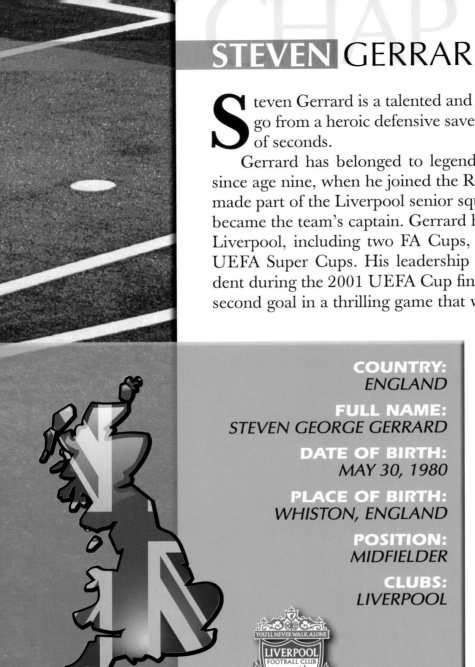

COUNTRY:
ENGLAND

FULL NAME:
STEVEN GEORGE GERRARD

DATE OF BIRTH:
MAY 30, 1980

PLACE OF BIRTH:
WHISTON, ENGLAND

POSITION:
MIDFIELDER

CLUBS:
LIVERPOOL

Steven Gerrard is a talented and vigorous midfielder who can go from a heroic defensive save to score a thriller in a matter of seconds.

Gerrard has belonged to legendary English team Liverpool since age nine, when he joined the Reds' youth academy. He was made part of the Liverpool senior squad in 1998, and in 2003, he became the team's captain. Gerrard has lifted many trophies with Liverpool, including two FA Cups, two League Cups, and two UEFA Super Cups. His leadership and inspiration became evident during the 2001 UEFA Cup final, when he scored the Reds' second goal in a thrilling game that was resolved in overtime and gave Liverpool their first European trophy in 17 years. Four years later, he helped inspire one of the greatest comebacks in soccer history, when Liverpool faced AC Milan in the UEFA Champions League final. By halftime, AC Milan had a commanding 3–0 lead, and Liverpool looked defeated. But then, Gerrard scored a header and lifted the team spirit in every play of the game. Liverpool scored two more goals in six minutes, forcing the game into overtime. After a penalty shoot-out, Gerrard lifted the cup for Liverpool and was named UEFA's most valuable player.

Gerrard is also a valuable member of England's national team, where he has played since May 2000. He was a substitute

during the EURO 2000 and was part of the English team that qualified for the 2002 World Cup. Unfortunately, a groin injury left him out of the competition. He scored a goal during the EURO 2004 and two more during World Cup 2006. But in both tournaments, England was eliminated by Portugal in the quarterfinals.

Steven Gerrard has played with his current club, Liverpool, since he was nine years old. With the English National team, he has been a steady force since 2000.

23

THIERRY HENRY

Fast, powerful, and a master in one-on-one situations, Thierry Henry is one of the most enjoyable players to watch on a soccer field.

Born of Antillean parents in the suburbs of Paris, Henry made his debut with Monaco in 1994, when he helped the team win

COUNTRY:
FRANCE

FULL NAME:
THIERRY DANIEL HENRY

DATE OF BIRTH:
AUGUST 17, 1977

PLACE OF BIRTH:
LES ULIS, ESSONNE, FRANCE

POSITION:
WINGER

CLUBS:
MONACO, JUVENTUS, ARSENAL, BARCELONA

CHAPTER 9

TIMELINE

1997: WON LIGUE 1 WITH MONACO.

1998: WON WORLD CUP WITH FRANCE.

1999: JOINED ARSENAL.

2004 AND 2005: WON EUROPEAN GOLDEN BOOT.

2006: WON HIS FIFTH FRENCH PLAYER OF THE YEAR AWARD.

2007: JOINED FC BARCELONA.

the Ligue 1 and the French Super Cup, and, more important, reach the semifinal in the UEFA Cup for the first time in the history of les Rouge et Blanc. An uneventful season with Italian powerhouse Juventus followed in 1998, but it was after his transfer to Arsenal in England that Thierry Henry became an international superstar.

While with the French national team, things moved swiftly for Henry, who had his first appearance with France at the age of 20. He scored three goals in the first two games of the 1998 World Cup and was a key element in the French squad that lifted the first World Cup trophy in the country's history. The champions quickly went on to win a second international tournament at the EURO 2000, with Henry ending the tournament as the team's top scorer. All this raised the expectations for the 2002 World Cup, but France and Henry failed to score a single goal in the tournament and exited the cup in the first round.

Meanwhile, the London climate seem to fit Henry, and his performance in Arsenal was nothing but impressive. He was the

Thierry Henry is shown during his days with the British team Arsenal, where he became an international soccer star.

25

team's top scorer four years in a row and was named European Golden Boot for two consecutive years. With Henry on the attack, Arsenal won two Premiership Leagues and three FA Cups. With 226 goals, he became Arsenal's all-time leader scorer. Arsenal fans were heartbroken when the team announced that Henry was leaving to join FC Barcelona in 2007. In a poll of Arsenal's 50 greatest players, conducted on the team's Web site in July 2008, Henry was picked as Arsenal's greatest player ever.

After the disastrous 2002 World Cup, Henry and France returned to the 2006 World Cup determined to regain international recognition. Henry scored three important goals and helped the team return to the final game against Italy. But France lost the game in penalty shoot-outs. Henry watched from the bench, since he had been substituted in extra time after his legs had cramped. In October 2007, Henry became France's top scorer of all time, passing team legend Michel Platini.

In 2009, Henry won the treble with Barcelona. This means that he won three major tournaments in the same year: the Spanish League, the Copa del Rey, and the UEFA Champions League.

CHAPTER 10

ZLATAN IBRAHIMOVIĆ

The son of a Bosnian father and a Croatian mother, Zlatan Ibrahimović was born in Sweden, where he is just as big a hero as he is in Italy.

Ibrahimović started playing soccer at age eight in the city of Malmö. He signed his first contract with Malmö FF in 1996 and started playing on the senior team three years after that. Soon, top teams came knocking at the door. French coach Arsène Wenger tried to get Ibrahimović for Arsenal in London, and legendary boss Leo Beenhakker tried to sign him with AFC Ajax in Holland. After a very public battle, Beenhakker prevailed and signed Ibrahimović with Ajax in 2001. Ibrahimović's style soon captured the imagination of Ajax fans, helping the team win two Eredivisie titles in 2002 and 2004.

By 2004, Ibrahimović's fame had passed Ajax's budget, and they were unable to keep him when Italian powerhouse Juventus opened their wallets for the Swedish striker. Ibrahimović scored 16 goals in his first season in Turin and proved to have the right skills to penetrate the tough Italian defenders. In 2005, he was named Guldbollen, or Swedish Footballer of the Year, for the first time, an honor he would win again in 2007 and 2008. In 2006,

COUNTRY:
SWEDEN

DATE OF BIRTH:
OCTOBER 3, 1981

PLACE OF BIRTH:
MALMÖ, SWEDEN

POSITION:
STRIKER

CLUBS:
MALMÖ, AJAX, JUVENTUS, INTERNAZIONALE

Ibrahimović left Turin to join their archrivals, Internazionale, in Milan. With Inter, his success kept growing and he became the team's top scorer in his first season. He also helped the team win two consecutive Serie A titles in 2007 and 2008.

Zlatan Ibrahimović kicks a ball during a game with Internationale de Milan. Ibrahimović is one of the most explosive and spectacular strikers in soccer.

Ibrahimović's club career has not matched his performances with the Swedish national team. The blue and yellow squad participated in the 2002 World Cup and again in 2006. Ibrahimović scored two goals in the EURO 2004, but he missed a key penalty shot and Sweden was sent home. The EURO 2008 held a similar fate, and after scoring two goals, Ibrahimović and Sweden were eliminated.

CHAPTER 11

KAKÁ

Meet Kaká, the total footballer. Not only can this Brazilian forward kick the ball with both feet, he is lethal with his head and has great speed, superior ball control, and impressive technique.

Ricardo Izecson dos Santos Leite was born in the Brazilian capital and moved to São Paulo at age seven. Kaká is a common term of

Kaká plays with legendary Italian team AC Milan during a UEFA Champions League match in 2006.

COUNTRY:
BRAZIL

FULL NAME:
RICARDO IZECSON DOS SANTOS LEITE

DATE OF BIRTH:
APRIL 22, 1982

PLACE OF BIRTH:
BRASÍLIA, BRAZIL

POSITION:
FORWARD

CLUBS:
SÃO PAULO, MILAN, REAL MADRID

TIMELINE

2001: *DEBUTED WITH SÃO PAULO.*

2002: *WON WORLD CUP WITH BRAZIL.*

2003: *JOINED AC MILAN.*

2007: *WON FIFA WORLD PLAYER OF THE YEAR AWARD.*

2007: *NAMED UEFA CHAMPIONS LEAGUE TOP SCORER.*

2008: *NAMED IN THE TIME 100 INFLUENTIAL PEOPLE LIST.*

2009: *JOINED REAL MADRID.*

endearment for the name "Ricardo" in Brazil, and this is what his younger brother started calling the future soccer star. Kaká signed his first professional contract with São Paulo at age 15. That year, he had a swimming accident that resulted in a spinal fracture, but against all odds, he made a complete recovery. Since then, Kaká has been a devout evangelical Christian, making headlines on many occasions by removing his jersey to reveal a T-shirt that says "I Belong to Jesus."

Kaká played 146 games with São Paulo, scoring more than 58 goals and helping the team win the 2001 Torneio Rio-São and the 2002 Campeonato Paulista. From the beginning of his career, Kaká received calls from top European clubs interested in signing him. In 2003, he finally agreed to be transferred to AC Milan, in Italy. The Brazilian had an immediate impact in the "Old Continent," scoring 10 goals in 30 games and winning the Italian Serie A and the European Super Cup, all in his first season.

When Brazil won the 2002 World Cup, Kaká was part of the team, but he played only 25 minutes. Three years later, he was a key player when Brazil conquered the 2005 Confederations Cup, scoring the second goal of the game in the final against Argentina.

Back with Milan, Kaká had another great year in 2006, scoring three hat tricks in one season, including one during the UEFA Champions League. These performances set the scene for the 2006 World Cup in Germany. Expectations were high after Kaká scored the winning goal in the opening match. Brazil and Kaká moved to the second round, but they did not play well. Brazil reached the quarterfinals, but they were eliminated by France.

In May 2007 with Milan, Kaká played the UEFA Champions League final against Liverpool. Kaká provided the assistance for Milan's second goal and won the most prestigious European tournament for the first time in his career. After playing his 200th match with Milan, Kaká won the Ballon d'Or and took home the FIFA Best World Player Award.

Kaká has been an ambassador for the United Nations World Food Programme

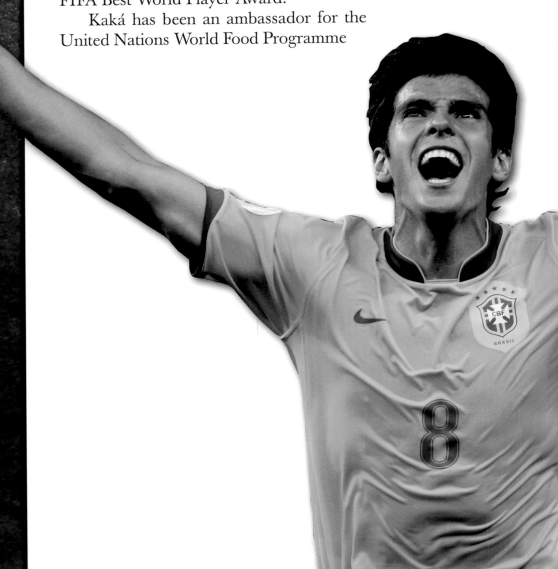

since 2004, and *Time* magazine named him one of the 100 Most Influential People of 2008, recognizing his work on and off the pitch.

In January 2009, many European clubs made bids to get Kaká in their lineups. The two highest bids came from British team Manchester City and Real Madrid in Spain. After long negotiations, Kaká signed a six-year contract with Real Madrid in June 2009. By joining Real Madrid, Kaká would have the opportunity to play in one of the best teams in the history of soccer and the winner of the title of the best soccer club of the 20th century.

Kaká celebrates scoring the opening goal during the World Cup Germany 2006 against Croatia. Known as the total footballer, Kaká is one of the most complete soccer players in history.

CHAPTER 12

MIROSLAV KLOSE

Miroslav Klose is the only player to have scored five or more goals in two consecutive World Cups. Not bad for a carpenter who was not even playing for a senior team two years before his first World Cup appearance. Klose was born in Poland and moved to Germany as a child in 1987. The family was following Miroslav's father, a professional Polish soccer player married to a member of the Polish women's national handball team. The family finally settled in Kusel, Germany.

In 1994, Klose joined the reserve team of FC Kaiserslautern while finishing an apprenticeship to become a carpenter. In 1999, he was promoted to the Kaiserslautern first team, where he started to get international attention. The Polish national team tried to persuade him to play for their side, but Klose wanted to take a chance and play for the three-time world-champion German national team. His gamble paid off, and he was called to play with Germany in 2001. A year later, he was playing his first World Cup. Klose's great speed, quick reactions, and superb aerial skills exploded, and he scored five goals in the tournament—all of them headers.

COUNTRY:
GERMANY

DATE OF BIRTH:
JUNE 9, 1978

PLACE OF BIRTH:
OPOLE, POLAND

POSITION:
STRIKER

CLUBS:
FC HOMBURG, FC KAISERSLAUTERN, WERDER BREMEN, BAYERN MUNICH

In 2004, Klose was transferred to Werder Bremen, one of the best teams in Germany. With Bremen, he scored 25 goals in 26 games and became the Bundesliga top scorer in 2005. He was back in the 2006 World Cup, and this time, he was playing in

Miroslav Klose scores a header with his club FC Bayern Munich in November 2008. Klose's rise from regional player to international star is considered one of the fastest in soccer history.

Germany. By then, Klose was a national hero. Again, he scored five goals. This time, only one was a header, and this was enough to earn him the Golden Shoe Award for the top scorer at the tournament.

In 2007, Klose joined one of the most prestigious teams in the world, Bayern Munich, and he won the Bundesliga in his first year with the team.

CHAPTER 13

RAFAEL MÁRQUEZ

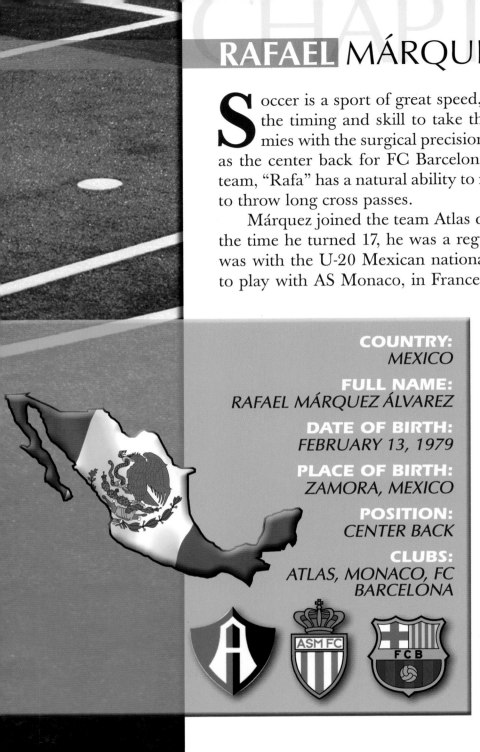

Soccer is a sport of great speed, and not many players have the timing and skill to take the ball away from their enemies with the surgical precision of Rafael Márquez. Playing as the center back for FC Barcelona and the Mexican national team, "Rafa" has a natural ability to read the game and the vision to throw long cross passes.

Márquez joined the team Atlas de Guadalajara at age 13. By the time he turned 17, he was a regular on the senior team and was with the U-20 Mexican national team. In 1999, Rafa went to play with AS Monaco, in France, where he won the Ligue 1 and the Super Cup. He was also named Best Defense Player of the Year. Márquez was also part of the Mexican national team that won the 1999 FIFA Confederations Cup against Brazil.

At age 23, Rafa was named captain for Mexico for the 2002 World Cup. After a great start, Mexico finished on top of Italy in the first round but lost their first game in the knockout stage, with Márquez leaving the field early after being shown a red card. Mexico beat Brazil again in the CONCACAF Gold Cup 2003, and Rafa scored a goal in the semifinals. In the 2006 World Cup in Germany, Rafa returned as captain. Mexico advanced to the second round, where they faced Argentina. At the sixth minute, Rafa scored with a powerful

COUNTRY:
MEXICO

FULL NAME:
RAFAEL MÁRQUEZ ÁLVAREZ

DATE OF BIRTH:
FEBRUARY 13, 1979

PLACE OF BIRTH:
ZAMORA, MEXICO

POSITION:
CENTER BACK

CLUBS:
ATLAS, MONACO, FC BARCELONA

header, but Argentina came back and beat Mexico in overtime.

In 2003, Rafa went to play with FC Barcelona in Spain, becoming only the second Mexican to play for the legendary team. Almost from the beginning, Rafa was one of the most regular players in Barcelona, and in 2005, he had a spectacular season that helped Barcelona win La Liga. The next year, Rafa won the UEFA Champions League with Barca, becoming the first Mexican player in history to win the most prestigious tournament in Europe.

Rafael Márquez is one of the most trusted defenders on the soccer field. Márquez's skill in anticipating the moves of rival players has been praised by many soccer experts.

CHAPTER 14

MARTA

Marta wanted so badly to be a soccer player that she actually traveled three days by bus to get to Vasco da Gama, her first club in Rio de Janeiro. But she was such a good player that the club paid all the expenses and helped her move in with relatives in Rio. Marta was 14 years old.

Life with Vasco da Gama didn't last long, as the team ended their women's team in 2001. But by then, Marta had finished as top scorer in a Brazilian youth tournament and won the Golden Ball in the FIFA U-20 Women's World Cup. After one season with club Santa Cruz in Brazil, she joined Umeå IK in Sweden, at age 18, where she found the net 63 times in her three first seasons.

Martha is a gifted left-footed midfielder who moves to the attacking position with great timing and vision. Her skills and ball control are so great that she often dribbles two or three players before passing the ball to her teammates. Although Marta was elected FIFA Best Player in the World in 2006, it was during the Pan American Games in Brazil that fans discovered her stunning game. Marta

COUNTRY:
BRAZIL

FULL NAME:
MARTA VIEIRA DA SILVA

DATE OF BIRTH:
FEBRUARY 19, 1986

PLACE OF BIRTH:
DOIS RIACHOS, ALAGOAS, BRAZIL

POSITION:
FORWARD

CLUBS:
VASCO DA GAMA, SANTA CRUZ, UMEÅ IK, LOS ANGELES SOL

Marta controls the ball during a match against Australia in the Women's World Cup 2007. Many think that Marta is the most exciting player in the history of women's soccer.

finished the tournament as top scorer, with 12 goals, and gave Brazil the gold medal. She was brilliant in the final game at the famous Maracanã stadium, where she was quickly compared to the legendary player Pelé.

Brazil and Marta reached the World Cup final for the first time in 2007. Although Brazil lost the final game against Germany, Marta had one of the most impressive individual performances in the history of the World Cup, scoring seven goals and taking home the Golden Ball Award as best player in the tournament and picking up her second award as FIFA Best Player in the World.

Following the World Cup, Marta returned to Umeå IK, where she helped the team win their fourth league title in four years. She also received her third FIFA World Player of the Year Award in three years. After four years in Sweden, Martha announced that she would move to the United States and play for the Los Angeles Sol in the new Women's Professional Soccer league.

LIONEL MESSI

Meet Lionel Messi, the next great soccer legend—that is, if injuries spare this soccer prodigy, who has impressed fans and rivals alike on any field where he has had a chance to show his skills.

Fast, smart, and bold, Messi can do anything with the ball. He started doing it at very young age. By the time he was five, people were talking about his talents. When he was eight, he was already playing for the school that had of one of the best teams in Argentina. Rumors of a kid who would become the next soccer star spread quickly beyond Argentina. However, at the age of 11, Messi was diagnosed with a growth hormone deficiency. His family couldn't afford the $1,500 a month that was needed for the treatment, and Argentinean teams were struggling with financial crises of their own. FC Barcelona in Spain knew of Messi's gift for soccer and offered to pay for the treatment if Messi and his family moved to Europe. Messi joined FC Barcelona at age 13.

Messi became the youngest player to play a league game with Barcelona, at the age of 17, during his debut in the 2004–2005

COUNTRY:
ARGENTINA

DATE OF BIRTH:
JUNE 24, 1987

PLACE OF BIRTH:
ROSARIO, ARGENTINA

POSITION:
SECOND STRIKER

CLUBS:
FC BARCELONA

season. In May 2005, he became the youngest player ever to score in a league game for Barcelona. Success continued with the Argentinean national during the 2005 FIFA World Youth Championship in the Netherlands. Argentina lifted the cup, and Messi was top scorer and best player of the tournament.

La Pulga (the Flea), as his teammates called him due to his small size and fast moves, was selected to play with the national

team during the 2006 World Cup, becoming the youngest player to represent Argentina at a World Cup. Messi scored a goal in a victory over Serbia and played in the next two games. But he was left on the bench in the quarterfinal game against Germany that ended Argentina's run.

The first of a series of injuries slowed Messi's rise to stardom, but they didn't stop him. He was on the injury list when Barcelona won the 2006 UEFA Champions League but came back strong the next season. He returned for a celebrated hat trick against Barcelona's archrivals, Real Madrid.

Since the beginning of his career, Messi has been compared with Argentinean legend Diego Armando Maradona. But it was Messi's goal against Getafe that brought all the comparisons to reality. Messi scored in an impressive run that started 203 feet (62 meters) from the goal, dribbling six players and kicking the ball softly into the net. The action was almost a copy of one of Maradona's goals in the 1986 World Cup, a goal that was billed as "The Goal of the Century."

Messi returned to international action during the 2007 Copa América. He had an impressive tournament and was named the best young player of the tournament. Although Argentina lost in the final against Brazil, fans will always remember Messi's goal during the semifinals against Mexico, when La Pulga floated the ball over the Mexican goalie to find the net.

The 2008 Olympics in Beijing were the next stop for Messi's greatness. He scored two goals and had two assists in Argentina's run to the final. In the gold medal match, he played his best soccer and helped Argentina defeat Nigeria 1–0. Lionel Messi was only 20 years old at the time.

Lionel Messi is sure to be the best player in the world for many years. Here, he dribbles two Nigerian defenders during the Olympic soccer final at the Beijing games in 2008. "La Pulga" won the gold medal for Argentina.

BIRGIT PRINZ

Franz Beckenbauer, Gerd Müller, and Lothar Matthäus have two things in common: they are German, and they are among the best footballers of all time. But the pantheon of German soccer would not be complete without the name of Birgit Prinz.

To start, let's consider her record: Women's World Cup winner in 2003 and 2007; Olympic bronze medalist in 2000, 2004, and 2008; four-time UEFA European Championship winner; German Champion League and German Cup winner on eight occasions; Germany Super Cup winner in 1996; and champion of the American Professional Championship, WUSA, in 2002. Prinz may not include in her résumé that she received, and declined, an offer from Italian team AC Perugia—a men's team in the Italian Serie A—but she certainly will highlight that she has been German Women's Footballer of the Year seven times and FIFA Women's World Player of the Year in 2003, 2004, and 2005.

Prinz was born in Frankfurt am Main and made her international debut at the age of 16. A natural striker with great speed and ball control, Prinz has broken every scoring record she has encountered. She is the all-time leading scorer in Women's World Cup history, with 13 career goals, and she has the all-time scoring record with the national team, with 116 goals in 173 games.

COUNTRY:
GERMANY

DATE OF BIRTH:
OCTOBER 25, 1977

PLACE OF BIRTH:
FRANKFURT AM MAIN, GERMANY

POSITION:
FORWARD

CLUBS:
FSV FRANKFURT, FFC FRANKFURT, CAROLINA COURAGE, FFC FRANKFURT

Birgit Prinz became the first player to be named the FIFA Women's World Player of the Year in three consecutive years: 2003, 2004, and 2005.

Prinz has also scored high off the field, actively participating in FIFA's campaign against racism, and she has visited children in war-affected areas in Afghanistan as a patron of the Learn and Play Project supported by FIFA, the National Olympic Committee, and Afghanistan Aid.

CHAPTER 17

RAÚL

Ask who Raúl González is in Madrid, and you will get thousands of answers. But simply ask for Raúl, and everybody will know that you are talking about a national hero—and one of the best forwards of all time.

Raúl has worked his entire life to become one of the most admired players in soccer by methodically building a career that goes beyond his goals or spectacular play. In a sport where talented players are lured from team to team by multimillion-dollar contracts, Raúl has made a point of spending his entire career with Real Madrid, where he has played since joining the youth team in 1992. Moreover, after more than 510 games with Real and more than 100 with the Spanish national team, Raúl has never seen a red card in his career.

Raúl became the youngest player to line up with Real Madrid in 1994, at 17 years and 4 months, scoring nine goals and lifting the La Liga trophy in his first season. Since then, he has won La Liga five more times and conquered the Pichichi award as Spain's top scorer in 1999 and 2001. Raúl is a fighter and one of the few strikers who can score in almost every way. Many of his goals may not be pretty, but they are the result of never giving up on a play. In February 2009, he scored his 312th career goal for Real Madrid, breaking the record of legendary player Alfredo di Stéfano.

In European competitions, Raúl has become a mythical player. He holds so many records that it would be impossible to mention

COUNTRY:
SPAIN

FULL NAME:
RAÚL GONZÁLEZ BLANCO

DATE OF BIRTH:
JUNE 27, 1977

PLACE OF BIRTH:
MADRID, SPAIN

POSITION:
FORWARD

CLUBS:
REAL MADRID

them all. He has won the UEFA Champions League three times and became the first player to score 50 goals in this competition, raising his tally to 64 by the 2009 tournament. He has played in 123 UEFA Champions matches, another record, and he is the only player in history to have scored in two UEFA Champions finals.

Raúl is the best scorer on the Spanish national team, with 44 goals. He helped Spain reach the semifinals of the 1995 FIFA World Youth Championship and has played in three World Cups—1998, 2002, and 2006—although without much success. A great controversy surrounded the decision of Spanish coach Luis Aragonés to leave Raúl out of the Spanish national team for the EURO 2008, when La Furia would become European champion. Raúl was openly upset about the decision, but he has promised to be back with the national team and break another record, or two.

CHAPTER 18

RONALDINHO

R onaldinho is Portuguese for "Little Ronaldo," and this soccer wizard really began to shine at a very young age. At age 13, he scored 23 goals in a single game, and he was a world champion before turning 17.

Ronaldinho's first team was Grêmio de Porto Alegre, and he was transferred to Paris

COUNTRY:
BRAZIL

FULL NAME:
RONALDO DE ASSIS MOREIRA

DATE OF BIRTH:
MARCH 21, 1980

PLACE OF BIRTH:
PORTO ALEGRE, BRAZIL

POSITION:
ATTACKING MIDFIELDER

CLUBS:
GRÊMIO, PARIS SAINT-GERMAIN, FC BARCELONA, AC MILAN

TIMELINE

1997: WON U-17 WORLD CUP WITH BRAZIL.

2001: JOINED PARIS SAINT-GERMAIN.

2002: WON THE WORLD CUP WITH BRAZIL.

2003: JOINED FC BARCELONA.

2004 AND 2005: NAMED FIFA BEST WORLD PLAYER AWARD.

2006: WON UEFA CHAMPIONS LEAGUE WITH BARCELONA.

2008: JOINED AC MILAN.

Saint-Germain, in France, in 2001. He played two uneventful years in Paris, in which his focus seemed to be on the Brazilian national team. After winning the U-17 World Cup in 1997, he conquered the 1999 Copa América and traveled to the 2002 World Cup in Japan/Korea as a rising soccer star. Ronaldinho didn't disappoint, becoming one of the best players in the tournament and helping Brazil to win their fifth World Cup title.

The soccer world was taken by surprise by Ronaldinho's skills, speed, and all-around exceptional talent, but it is his great smile and joy of playing the game that have made him a fan favorite. He made international headlines when, in 2003, he joined FC Barcelona, a team that helped him showcase his best soccer yet. In his first two seasons with Barcelona, he won the La Liga trophy twice, and by 2004, he was named FIFA World Player of the Year, a feat he repeated a year later. That

---

Ronaldinho is among the five Brazilian players who have won the FIFA Best World Player Award since the trophy was established in 1991. Ronaldinho has won twice, in 2004 and 2005.

same year, Ronaldinho won his first Confederation Cup with Brazil, and in 2006, he lifted the UEFA Champions League with Barcelona.

By the end of 2006, Ronaldinho had won every major soccer tournament on the planet. Unfortunately, the talented Brazilian failed to make an impression during the 2006 World Cup, and he was not included in the Brazilian team that won the Copa América 2007. Ronaldinho's smile began to fade. He clearly needed a change, and Italian powerhouse AC Milan was up for the challenge. Ronaldinho joined Milan in 2008 and quickly became a starting player with the Rossoneri ("Red-blacks").

Ronaldinho joined Milan on a three-year contract. With the number 10 already taken by teammate Clarence Seedorf, Ronaldinho selected the unusual number 80 for his jersey because he was born in 1980. With Brazilian teammate Kaká having left Milan in June 2009, Ronaldinho has been called to lead the Italian team to soccer glory.

Ronaldinho, wearing the AC Milan colors, heads the ball during an Italian Serie A match. Ronaldinho's talent and joy of the game make him a fan favorite.

CRISTIANO RONALDO

Born in Madeira, Portugal, Cristiano Ronaldo started playing soccer when he was 9 years old, and at age 15, he had a scare that threatened to end his soccer dreams. While playing with the youth team of Sporting CP, he was diagnosed with a racing heart. Ronaldo underwent successful laser surgery and was back to training in a matter of days.

After his debut with the Sporting senior team in 2001, Ronaldo caught the attention of many important

In 2009, Cristiano Ronaldo became the first player from Manchester United to win the FIFA Best World Player award.

COUNTRY:
PORTUGAL

DATE OF BIRTH:
FEBRUARY 5, 1985

PLACE OF BIRTH:
FUNCHAL, MADEIRA, PORTUGAL

POSITION:
WINGER

CLUBS:
SPORTING CP (PORTUGAL), MANCHESTER UNITED (ENGLAND), REAL MADRID (SPAIN)

TIMELINE

1997: *JOINED SPORTING CP AT THE AGE OF 12.*

2003: *BECAME FIRST PORTUGUESE PLAYER TO JOIN MANCHESTER UNITED.*

2006: *WON FIRST OF TWO CONSECUTIVE PREMIER LEAGUE CHAMPIONSHIPS WITH MANCHESTER UNITED.*

2008: *WITH MANCHESTER UNITED WON THE UEFA CHAMPIONS LEAGUE; WON THE BALLON D'OR AWARD.*

2009: *RONALDO IS UNINJURED IN A CAR ACCIDENT WHILE DRIVING HIS FERRARI 599 GTB; IS NAMED FIFA WORLD PLAYER OF THE YEAR; JOINS REAL MADRID.*

teams, but it was the legendary club Manchester United that finally signed him in 2003, at age 18. Ronaldo became the first Portuguese to join the celebrated British squad, and he promptly showed that he was the right man for the challenge. He won FIFPro Young Player of the Year two years in a row and helped Man U win the Premiership League in 2007 and 2008.

Ronaldo has been a staple of the Portuguese national team since his debut in August 2003. Portugal was the host of the EURO 2004, where Ronaldo scored two goals and helped his side reach the final against Greece. But Ronaldo and Portugal failed to score against the Greek defensive game and lost 1–0. Two years later, Portugal, with Ronaldo, proved to be one of the most spectacular teams in the 2006 World Cup. They reached the quarterfinals against England, where Ronaldo had to face many Manchester United players. One incident in particular, with teammate Wayne Rooney, infuriated the English fans, who

accused Ronaldo of influencing the referee to show a red card to Rooney. Portugal won the game but finished the tournament in fourth place.

The English fans and the sports press blamed Ronaldo for the team's elimination, and it looked like his career with Manchester United would have to come to an end. But the Man U coaches and some teammates, including Rooney, urged Ronaldo to stay.

In 2008, Ronaldo made many of his childhood dreams come true, first by playing the UEFA Champions League final against archrivals Chelsea. Ronaldo scored with an impressive header in the 26th minute of the game, but Chelsea tied the score in the final minutes of the first half. The championship had to be decided in a penalty shoot-out. Ronaldo missed his shot, but two Chelsea players missed, too, giving Manchester United their third UEFA Champions League title. A few weeks later, Ronaldo became the first Man U player to win the European Footballer of the Year Award in 40 years. And if that wasn't enough, he received the 2008 FIFA World Player of the Year Award, becoming the second Portuguese player, and the first ever from Manchester United, to receive the distinction.

In the spring of 2009, the soccer world was shaken when Spanish team Real Madrid announced that Cristiano Ronaldo was leaving Manchester United to join the Spanish squad for a record-breaking transfer of $132 million. The transfer made Cristiano Ronaldo the most expensive player in soccer history. As if that wasn't enough, Real Madrid hired Brazilian superstar Kaká to form with Ronaldo what is sure to be one of the most impressive attacks in the history of soccer.

Cristiano Ronaldo lifts the FIFA World Club Cup in December 2008 at the Yokohama International Stadium in Japan. Manchester United beat LDU Quito of Ecuador in the final match.

CHAPTER 20

FERNANDO TORRES

Fernando Torres scored the goal that took Spain to soccer glory. It happened during the EURO 2008 final against Germany. Spain has been a powerful soccer nation since the beginning of the 20th century, and Spanish clubs such as Real Madrid and Barcelona are among the best. However, La Furia had won only one important international title, and that was in the EURO 1964. All that changed when Torres used his speed to win a ball over a German defender and scored the goal that gave Spain the European championship.

At age seven, Torres started playing soccer as a goalkeeper, but after an accident that left him with some broken teeth, his mother urged him to change his position. Torres may have lost a few teeth, but soccer won a fantastic striker. He joined Atletico de Madrid at age 11, and he debuted in the second division in 2001. By then, he had won the UEFA, U-16, and UEFA U-19, finishing as the tournament top scorer each time. By age 19, Torres was Atletico's captain and became known as El Niño, or "the Kid."

Torres played in the 2006 World Cup with Spain, scoring three goals and giving Spain a promising start. But Spain couldn't keep the momentum and lost their second-round game against France. La Furia was sent home, but El Niño had made such a good impression that many European teams scrambled to sign the powerful striker. Liverpool, one of the most successful clubs in England, had the

COUNTRY:
SPAIN

DATE OF BIRTH:
MARCH 20, 1984

PLACE OF BIRTH:
MADRID, SPAIN

POSITION:
STRIKER

CLUBS:
ATLETICO DE MADRID, LIVERPOOL

"El Niño," Fernando Torres, holds the trophy after winning the EURO 2008 championship against Germany in Vienna, Austria, in June 2008. Torres scored the winning goal on a play of great speed and skill.

best offer, and Torres signed with his new team in March 2008. In his first year with the Reds, Torres established a new record for the most prolific foreign goal scorer in a debut season with Liverpool, scoring 24 times. After only a year and a half with the team, he was included in a list published by the *Times of London*, as one of the 50 greatest Liverpool players.

GLOSSARY

African Cup of Nations The main international soccer competition for national teams in Africa.

Bundesliga The top level in Germany's soccer league system.

CONCACAF Gold Cup The main soccer competition of the national soccer teams governed by CONCACAF (Confederation of North, Central America and Caribbean Association Football).

Copa América The main tournament of the men's national soccer teams in South America and selected teams from North America.

Copa del Rey An annual cup competition where Spanish teams from first and second divisions play each other.

EURO The UEFA European Football Championship, commonly known as EURO, is a soccer tournament contested by European nations every four years.

European Footballer of the Year Also known as the "Ballon d'Or," an award given by international journalists to the player who has been considered to be the best in Europe. Since 2007, the award considers players participating in any league in the world.

FA Cup A knockout cup competition in English soccer.

FIFA Fédération Internationale de Football Association, or Federation of Association Football; the international governing body of soccer.

Golden Ball Award A trophy given to the best player in a World Cup.

Intercontinental Cup Competition Contested between the winners of the European Cup and the South American Copa Libertadores.

La Liga The first division league in Spain; players in La Liga compete against the top professional clubs.

MLS Cup The annual championship game of Major League Soccer.

MLS Golden Boot An award given for the leading scorer in the Major League Soccer league.

Premier League The English professional league for the country's top clubs.

treble In soccer, this term describes the achievement of winning three top-tier trophies in one season.

UEFA The Union of European Football Associations is the administrative body for European soccer.

American Youth Soccer Organization
National Support and Training Center
12501 S. Isis Avenue
Hawthorne, CA 90250
(800) 872-2976
Web site: http://soccer.org/home.aspx
This organization administers youth recreational soccer leagues all over the country.
    Any skill level is welcome.

Canadian Soccer Association
Place Soccer Canada
237 rue Metcalfe Street
Ottawa, ON K2P 1R2
Canada
(613) 237-7678
E-mail: mini@soccercan.ca
Web site: http://www.canadasoccer.com
The Canadian Soccer Association works to promote soccer and improve the game at
    both the national and international levels.

CONCACAF
725 Fifth Avenue, Floor 17
New York, NY 10022
(212) 308-0044
E-mail: contact@concacaf.org
Web site: http://www.concacaf.com
With 40 member countries, the Confederation of North, Central America and
    Caribbean Association Football oversees soccer for these regions. It is one of six
    divisions of FIFA.

FIFA
FIFA-Strasse 20

P.O. Box 8044
Zurich, Switzerland
Web site: http://www.fifa.com
FIFA is the international organization that oversees soccer at the professional level. It
    sponsors the World Cup.

National Soccer Hall of Fame
18 Stadium Circle
Oneonta, NY 13820
(607) 432-3351
E-mail: nshof@soccerhall.org
Web site: http://www.soccerhall.org
The National Soccer Hall of Fame preserves and promotes the history of soccer in the
    United States.

U.S. Soccer Federation
1801 S. Prairie Avenue
Chicago, IL 60616
(312) 808-1300
Web site: http://www.ussoccer.com
The U.S. Soccer Federation oversees both professional and amateur soccer and helps to
    promote and develop the sport.

WEB SITES

Due to the changing nature of Internet links, Rosen Publishing has developed an online
list of Web sites related to the subject of this book. This site is updated regularly. Please
use this link to access the list:

http://www.rosenlinks.com/wsb/supe

Buckley, James. *Pelé*. New York, NY: DK Children, 2007.

Buxton, Ted. *Soccer Skills: For Young Players*. Buffalo, NY: Firefly Books, 2007.

Esckilsen, Erik. *Offsides*. New York, NY: Houghton Mifflin Books for Children, 2004.

Gifford, Clive. *The Kingfisher Soccer Encyclopedia*. New York, NY: Kingfisher, 2006.

Hornby, Hugh. *Soccer*. New York, NY: DK Children, 2008.

Hunt, Chris. *The Complete Book of Soccer*. Buffalo, NY: Firefly Books 2006.

Lisi, Clemente Angelo. *A History of the World Cup: 1930–2006*. Lanham, MD: Scarecrow Press, Inc., 2007.

Miers, Charles, and Elio Trifari, eds. *Soccer!: The Game and the World Cup*. New York, NY: Rizzoli International Publications, 1994.

Poulton, J. Alexander. *World's Greatest Soccer Players: Today's Hottest Superstars*. Montreal, Quebec: Overtime, 2006.

Radnedge, Keir. *The Complete Encyclopedia of Soccer*. London, England: Carlton Books, 2000.

Rigby, Robert. *Goal!: The Dream Begins*. New York, NY: Harcourt Paperbacks, 2006.

Stewart, Mark. *The World Cup*. New York, NY: Franklin Watts (Scholastic), 2003.

Weiland, Matt, and Sean Wilsey, eds. *The Thinking Fan's Guide to the World Cup*. New York, NY: HarperCollins Publishers, 2006.

Whitfield, David. *World Cup*. New York, NY: Weigl Publishers, 2007.

BIBLIOGRAPHY

BBC.com. "Pelé's List of the Greatest." Retrieved April 3, 2009 (http://news.bbc.co.uk/sport2/hi/football/3533891.stm).

ExpertFootball.com. "Soccer Styles of Play." Retrieved February 28, 2009 (http://expert-football.com/coaching/styles.php).

FIFA.com. "The History of FIFA." Retrieved February 28, 2009 (http://www.fifa.com/classicfootball/history/fifa/historyfifa1.html).

FIFA.com. "Previous FIFA World Cups." Retrieved February 22, 2009 (http://www.fifa.com/worldcup/archive/index.html).

Fiore, Fernando. *The World Cup: The Ultimate Guide to the Greatest Sports Spectacle in the World.* New York, NY: HarperCollins Publishers, 2006.

Hunt, Chris. *The Complete Book of Soccer.* Buffalo, NY: Firefly Books, 2006.

Lisi, Clemente Angelo. *A History of the World Cup: 1930–2006.* Lanham, MD: Scarecrow Press, Inc., 2007.

Miers, Charles, and Elio Trifari, eds. *Soccer!: The Game and the World Cup.* New York, NY: Rizzoli International Publications, 1994.

Montague, James. "Arsenal's Adebayor Wins Top African Honor." CNN.com. Retrieved March 26, 2009 (http://www.cnn.com/2009/SPORT/football/02/11/african.footballer/index.html?eref=rss_world).

Platini, Michel. "Quotes." MichelPlatini.org. Retrieved March 3, 2009 (http://www.michelplatini.org/Quotes.html).

Radnedge, Keir. *The Complete Encyclopedia of Soccer.* London, England: Carlton Books, 2000.

Rollings, Grant. "Heart Op That Saved Ronaldo." *Sun,* January 29, 2009. Retrieved March 20, 2009 (http://www.thesun.co.uk/sol/homepage/news/article2185215.ece).

Weiland, Matt, and Sean Wilsey, eds. *The Thinking Fan's Guide to the World Cup.* New York, NY: HarperCollins Publishers, 2006.

INDEX

A

AC Milan, 11, 22, 31, 32, 51
AC Perugia, 44
African Cup of Nations, 7, 20
African Footballer of the Year, 6, 17, 20, 21
Ajax, 28
Aragonés, Luis, 47
Arsenal, 6, 25, 27, 28

B

Baggio, Robert, 12
Bayern Munich, 15, 35
Black Stars, 18, 19

C

Chelsea, 16, 18
Confederation of North, Central America
    and Caribbean Association Football
    (CONCACAF), 36

E

EURO competitions, 9, 23, 25, 29, 53, 56

F

FC Barcelona, 21, 27, 36, 37, 41, 49, 56
Fédération Internationale de Football
    Association (FIFA), 12, 20, 32, 36, 38, 40,
    41, 43, 44, 45, 47, 49, 55

J

Juventus, 12, 13, 25, 28

L

La Liga, 11, 21, 37, 46, 49
Liverpool, 22, 32, 56, 57
Los Angeles Galaxy, 11, 14, 15

M

Manchester United, 8–9, 53, 55
Maradona, Diego Armando, 43

O

Olympic Games, 14, 43, 44

P

Pelé, 40
Pichichi award, 46
Platini, Michel, 27

R

Real Madrid, 11, 20, 33, 43, 46, 55, 56

S

São Paulo, 31
Seedorf, Clarence, 51
Serie A, 12, 13, 28, 31, 44
Stéfano, Alfredo di, 46

U

UEFA competitions, 6, 9, 12, 21, 22, 25, 32, 37,
    43, 44, 47, 51, 55, 56
Umeå IK, 38, 40

W

Werder Bremen, 34

ABOUT THE AUTHOR

Mauricio Velázquez de León is a writer and editor living in New York City. A passionate soccer fan, he has seen two World Cups live, one UEFA Champions League, and thousands of matches on television.

PHOTO CREDITS

Cover, p. 1 (left) Jamie McDonald/Getty Images, cover, pp. 1 (middle), 32–33 Alex Livesey/Getty Images; cover, p. 1 (right) Jeff Gross/Getty Images; pp. 4–5 Paul Ellis/AFP/Getty Images; p. 7 Pius Utomi Ekpei/AFP/Getty Images; pp. 8, 10 Ross Kinnaird/Getty Images; p. 13 Clive Mason/Getty Images; p. 15 Mike Ehrmann/Getty Images; p. 17 Shaun Botterill/Getty Images; p. 19 Michael Steele/Getty Images; p. 21 Jasper Juinen/Getty Images; p. 23 Ryan Pierse/Getty Images; pp. 24, 26 Denis Doyle/Getty Images; p. 29 Guiseppe Cacace/AFP/Getty Images; p. 30 Lars Baron/Bongarts/Getty Images; p. 35 Alexander Hassenstein/Bongarts/Getty Images; p. 37 Friedemann Vogel/Bongarts/Getty Images; p. 39 Goh Chai Hin/AFP/Getty Images; p. 42 Fabrice Coffrini/AFP/Getty Images; p. 45 Vladimir Rys/ Bongarts/Getty Images; p. 47 Pedro Armestre/AFP/Getty Images; p. 48 Stuart Franklin/Bongarts/Getty Images; p. 50 Damien Meyer/AFP/Getty Images; p. 52 Hamish Blair/Getty Images; p. 54 Matthew Peters/Manchester United/Getty Images; p. 57 Paul Ellis/AFP/Getty Images; page backgrounds and borders © www.istockphoto.com/Roberta Casaliggi.

Designer: Matthew Cauli; Editor: Bethany Bryan;
Photo Researcher: Cindy Reiman